PRAISE FOR JACQUELINE PIRTLE

Jacqueline takes you always directly to what you are ready to see or experience.

— LONGTIME CLIENT AND READER

It is liberating to face your own blocks and to be finally free of the weight that they have caused for many years. And while for me the changes I'm experiencing are noticeable and real, I still feel like myself. Just a more sure self.

— LONGTIME CLIENT AND READER

Jacqueline makes me BELIEVE I can be and live a joyful and magical existence every new day of my life!

— LONGTIME CLIENT AND READER

JACQUELINE PIRTLE

OPEN

Where it all starts!

A 30 day journal

COPYRIGHT

Copyright © 2021 Jacqueline Pirtle
www.FreakyHealer.com

All rights reserved. No part of this book may be reproduced or transmitted in any form or by any means, electronic or mechanical, including photocopying, recording, or by any information storage and retrieval system without the written permission of the publisher, except where permitted by law.

ISBN-13: 978-1-955059-08-4

Publisher: Freaky Healer

Editor-in-chief: Zoe Pirtle
All-round Support: Mitch Pirtle

Book cover design by Kingwood Creations kingwoodcreations.com

Author photo courtesy of Lionel Madiou madious.com

I want to let you know that all my books and holistic practitioner work together are a wholesome system, supporting you to live a more conscious, mindful, and happier life.

However, I made it so you can receive the benefit of living more joyously solely by working through this terrific journal book, while also experiencing the full satisfaction in continuing on to the next journal of this series—not to mention the rock solid tools you get by reading any of my other books or adding in my podcast *The Daily Freak*. Either way, I know you'll love my inspirational teachings.

Find out more:
www.freakyhealer.com
Amazon Author Page
The Daily Freak Podcast

So before you dive in, I want to thank you for hopping on the magic train with me! I truly hope you enjoy ***Open*** as much as I loved writing it, and if you do, it would be wonderful if you could take a short minute and leave a review on Amazon.com and Goodreads.com as soon as you can.

Your kind feedback helps other readers find my books easier, and be happy faster. Consider it a happy deed for the world.

Thank you!

ACKNOWLEDGMENTS

Let's be honest here… I have a dream team!

I could not have finished this book without the help of talented, creative, high-for-life, and phenomenal professionals.

From the bottom of my heart, I want to thank Zoe Pirtle for her editorial mastery; Mitch Pirtle for his all-round support; kingwoodcreations.com for their fun and polished book cover design; and madiouART.com for an amazing photo shoot.

I'd also like to extend a huge "Thank You!" to all the fans of my work and books—I created this beautiful journal series for you.

Life is spectacular with you on my side!

*If you ever wondered what would change for you if you were to BE and live **open** to the full extent of experiencing a vivid life, then you came to the right place!*

"I got you covered," says this journal book!

DEDICATION

*I dedicate this journal to all **closed** beings or things and challenge them to become **open**!*

INTRODUCTION

Incredible *open-uppers*,

I'm over the moon happy to be on this journey with you - connected and together - to mindfully and consciously create a better life for yourself and others—since you share your well-feeling with everything and everyone at all times. Just think of the power you have!

Everything is energy - you, me, this journal, your *open-ness*, and also *your closed-ness* - it's all one and the same: Energy!

It's also all connected and sharing at all times—meaning that you, your *blockages* and what they represent, and also the *open-ness* you will create with this journal, are all *one* and part of your wonderful being.

As these energies, everything, and everyone vibrates in different frequencies. Some are high like being **open**, and some are lower like being closed-up.

When you are **open** you are in a high value frequency because you go with the **open** flow of life and feel good since that essence represents living freely, forward, and resistance-free. In that *open-ness* is where you can truly be you, hear your inner guidance

INTRODUCTION

clearly, and can make your wishes, dreams, and desires come true.

Focusing on being *open* while dreaming about unlimited possibilities and thinking and feeling your dreams vividly - as alive - is a spectacular way of being.

In comparison, when you put all focus on your traumatic experiences that you have had, you are vibrating in a lower frequency because trauma feels like pain, sadness, anger, unhappiness, resentment, disbelief, and somewhat being unfortunate in life—clearly a state of being *closed* to well-being.

Sure, you can dwell on your hold-ups in life and get all deep into the *why* and *what*, letting them keep a tight grip on you and your life, but you can also take another road and shift your focus to your aligned *open-ness* while giving that magic the energetic momentum.

Know that you have the capability to get these closed patches so incredibly wide open - turning them inside out into an *openness* you never knew is possible - and feeling amazing by enjoying a healing of immense proportion.

Being *open* to all that life has in store for you is **where it all starts** because it allows unlimited opportunities to arrive in that wideness, since they can catch a hold of you until you hear - or sense - them loud and clear. Just think of that incredible match-up and shift into the higher frequency of happiness by being *one* with the excitement of these opportunities and manifestations. It's an automatic shot into being and living the best version of you—while changing at a constant and vivid speed, the way life naturally happens.

I say replace your *closed-ness* with your undeniable *open-ness* —boldly and widely living your life fully!

Journaling through this 30 day journal of **Open** will bring huge change by creating exactly *that* open space, where new magic can BE for you.

For every day in this book, there is a profound *opening* entry,

INTRODUCTION

inviting you to shift yourself into feeling amazing by journaling about your thoughts—creating a huge wide essence of love, peace, happiness, appreciation, respect, gratitude, acceptance for yourself, your life, and your truth which you will share with everything and everyone.

You will feel your utmost excitement and awe of everything being possible—of you being deserving and in charge of how your life IS and unfolds and what's included or excluded fully. Plus you will become a master in feeling phenomenal and manifesting what you want, all while learning to open up, live more consciously and mindfully, and become happier. A change that is forever!

As a side note, there are a couple bonus days at the end; in case you ever find the need to do two in a day, or to keep working while you wait for the next journal in this series to arrive. I also left you a few blank *Open-ness IS* pages to journal about additional ways to open yourself to your deepest wishes and dreams as they come in and up for you.

Enough chit-chat, I know you are ready, so grab your pen and have incredible fun with catching more life than you have ever caught, in your new open ways.

Happiest,
    Jacqueline

 Day 1

IMAGINE A BEAUTIFUL, wide, tall, gigantic door with the most gorgeous handle that you have ever seen. What's the visual you get—what color is your door and what shape is the handle? Now see yourself standing in front of that incredibly exciting door, grabbing that magic handle, and without any expectations - rather, simply in wonder - opening this spectacular wide portal. Wow! What an experience! Feel your curiosity of what's behind. Do you have goose-bumps yet? Can you feel the wide opening of yourself to whatever this practice has in store for you—the opening shift, the exciting energy, and the unlimited possibilities that could be? Go on, this is your cue to put into words what this opening act means for you! Most importantly, focus only on the aperture, don't head through the door yet, because tomorrow you'll continue the journey into what's beyond your magical door.

_____
_____
_____
_____
_____
_____
_____
_____
_____
_____
_____
_____

Open - Where it all starts!

 ay 2

WELCOME back to your magnificent door, that you opened wide and big—to be specific, you are at the exact split-second when the door is opening and you are in wonder of what's behind. Feel your whole being - your physical body, mind, soul, and your consciousness - opening up, just like that door. Now step through that open portal into your new open space! Breathe into the excitement and in-aweness of what you see on the other side. What's there in your magic world? How do you feel being there? What and who do you want in this new open space of yours? What magic is waiting and asking for your attention?

_____
_____
_____
_____
_____
_____
_____
_____
_____
_____
_____
_____
_____
_____
_____
_____

Open - Where it all starts!

Day 3

Now that you have taken the leap through your fantastic door and are living in your wide open essence, it's time to acknowledge that everything and everyone in your life - the good, bad, beautiful, and ugly, as we so wonderfully say - are always a chance to open up even more; to your magic, healing, betterment, expansion, and calibration into being and living the higher version of you. Knowing this, what will change for you? How will you live differently? What are your expectations for yourself and others when living focused on everything always being a gift?

Open - Where it all starts!

 Day 4

IN ORDER TO keep expanding beyond what you opened up to in the last few journal entries, we need to talk about what further open-ness is to you? How does it look, feel, sound, taste, and smell? What thoughts match it? What activities or practices represent you being more open? What words are you newly going to use and what lifestyle equals being more open?

___

Open - Where it all starts!

 ay 5

To get you the clarity of the difference between you being wide open or closed, we need to put a small little spotlight onto what being closed feels like for you. So without going too deep into the negative or state of unwell-feeling, what does it mean to be closed? How does it feel when you are closed? Where in your life, body, emotions, or mind, do you feel such a closed sensation? How will you rip it open and also have it stay open?

_____
_____
_____
_____
_____
_____
_____
_____
_____
_____
_____
_____
_____
_____
_____
_____
_____
_____
_____
_____

Open - Where it all starts!

ay 6

An open heart is a ____ heart! Fill in the blank with a positive flair, then feel and breathe into your heart. Sense it opening up, letting your humongous love flow out and in, while opening wider and wider. How does this feel? What kind of new day, and life, will this open heart practice create for you? Are you smiling yet?

Open - Where it all starts!

 Day 7

OPEN UP TO YOUR FORCES! What does that look like for you? How do your forces feel? What are your forces? Pick some you would like to open up to. What do your forces do for your life, body, mind, soul, and for the world?

Open - Where it all starts!

 ay 8

IN ORDER TO get what you want, you need to be open and allow what you want to come skipping through the door of life. What is the one thing right now that you desperately wish for? How will you open up to allow this dream of yours to arrive? Hint—copy and paste that practice on to the next, and then the next, thing that you are dreaming of!

_____
_____
_____
_____
_____
_____
_____
_____
_____
_____
_____
_____
_____
_____
_____
_____
_____
_____
_____
_____
_____

Open - *Where it all starts!*

 ay 9

AN OPEN MIND IS A ___ mind! Fill in the blank with what fits for you. What thoughts that you have feel closed to you being happy, healthy, energized, and vivid? What is the opposite of those closed thoughts—the open version of them? Make your list and add how you feel when shifting like that!

Open - Where it all starts!

 ay 10

LITTLE MESSAGES, signs, and wisdom are always available for you. Some are big and bold and in your face, while others are tiny and more hidden—but they are never not there. How will you open yourself to consciously catch all that help while you can, and while they are there? What's your magic trick?

Open - Where it all starts!

# Day 11

FOR SOLUTIONS TO come in and up you have to be open to receive and allow them to be. List the problems, hardships, or issues that are on your mind—refrain from digging deep here. How can you open up to the goodness in those happenings? How can you allow the invitation for change to happen in your life openly? How will you open up here?

_____
_____
_____
_____
_____
_____
_____
_____
_____
_____
_____
_____
_____
_____
_____
_____
_____
_____
_____
_____

Open - Where it all starts!

 ay 12

AN OPEN BODY IS A ____ body! Fill in the blank and feel into your physical body, into its energy. Where do you catch closed-up patches, blockages? Is there any pain, sadness, anger, or gunky energy somewhere? How will you shift those locked gates to be wide open portals to health, energy, and well-being?

___

Open - Where it all starts!

 ay 13

YOUR HEART WANTS you to open up to its guidance and to what it has to say—without ever questioning it. How will you openly and trustingly follow your heart more often?

Open - Where it all starts!

Day 14

OPENING up to all your feelings - and not only loving the ones you like - means you allow yourself to be wholesome and complete, also as-is. How loving of you! What feelings are you already welcoming with open arms, and which ones not? How will you change that?

_____
_____
_____
_____
_____
_____
_____
_____
_____
_____
_____
_____
_____
_____
_____
_____
_____
_____
_____
_____
_____
_____
_____
_____

Open - Where it all starts!

 ay 15

To let go of all your unfitting and old beliefs you have to be open enough to let them disappear—because if you are closed, they will stay behind a locked door. What old habits are you wanting to "poof" be gone? How will you open up and let them fly away?

_____
_____
_____
_____
_____
_____
_____
_____
_____
_____
_____
_____
_____
_____
_____
_____
_____
_____
_____
_____
_____

Open - Where it all starts!

 ay 16

CONGRATULATIONS, you have done quite some shifting so far! From this new open-ness, what does an open alignment with who you really are look like now? I bet it is very different than when you started your journey with **Open**. How will you stand up for this newfound you and *BE and live* as such?

_____
_____
_____
_____
_____
_____
_____
_____
_____
_____
_____
_____
_____
_____
_____
_____
_____
_____
_____

Open - Where it all starts!

 ay 17

LIVING a full life means that you spread your wings wide and far —welcomingly embracing everything that is there for you at all times. This asks for your full trust, because having only half the trust gets you only half the adventure. How will you openly receive your life in its full bloom? What activities, inspirations, and flavors are involved in such a wondrous lifestyle?

Open - Where it all starts!

Day 18

DO YOU LIKE CHANGE? If yes, what kind of change would feel good right now? How will you open up so it can actually arrive? If no, what's blocking you to allow a shift—and how will you get your behind into an open-ness where different can be?

_____
_____
_____
_____
_____
_____
_____
_____
_____
_____
_____
_____
_____
_____
_____
_____
_____
_____
_____
_____
_____
_____
_____

Open - Where it all starts!

 ay 19

CATCH your closed-up patches - your blockages - right now! Feel and sense into your physical body, your thoughts and feelings, your life, and your energy. Where are they—is there any physical symptom, emotional distress, or energetic impurity present? How will you shift those tight essences to be wide open again —*again* because once upon a time, they were?

___

Open - Where it all starts!

 ay 20

You know that crazy and unexplained inner voice of yours? Can you hear it? What is it saying? It takes your full open-ness to listen and follow its wisdom without ever questioning it. Are you that open? Are you that crazy? I hope I hear a "Yes!" Now how are you going to make sure that you stay that attentive?

___

Open - Where it all starts!

 ay 21

ARE you fully open to love? I'm not just talking about finding the love of your life—or having already found it. I'm bringing up the the essence, the energy, the feeling of love that is in your heart. Are you freely allowing the whole potential of love to flow through you? Are you willingly, and in a super-human style, ripping your chest open to welcome all love? Take a moment of reflection and write about how your incredible love feels for you, and what it is capable of! What is your letting-in-love plan?

_____
_____
_____
_____
_____
_____
_____
_____
_____
_____
_____
_____
_____
_____
_____
_____
_____
_____
_____
_____

Open - Where it all starts!

 ay 22

BEING open to new ways of nourishing your physical body means that you are keeping up with your ever changing physics. What foods are not really fitting anymore? What new foods, fresh cuisine, and different tastes could you give a try? Or is it the timing and amounts that could use a change-up?

Open - Where it all starts!

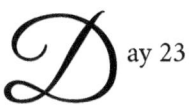 ay 23

MONEY! It's a gift from the heavens until it brings up negative, unhelpful, and downing feelings. Isn't that so? It takes lots of open-ness to allow the bounty of gold to arrive in unlimited fashion—because just like a shut door or one with only a peephole, not much will get through if you are closed. It also takes a loving attitude towards money because why else would money want to meet up with you? How are you going to manage a high-for-life attitude towards abundance—and how will you make sure you stay that way?

Open - Where it all starts!

 ay 24

EVERYTHING IS ALWAYS present in life; the negative and the positive, the ugly and the beautiful, the hurtful and the helpful, the wanted and the unwanted, and magic or no magic. To think that you are an open door letting in whatever you are focusing on puts in perspective where your focal point needs to be. What will you be more open to? What do you want to let into your life?

___

Open - Where it all starts!

Day 25

IN ORDER TO stop judging yourself and others, you have to be open to realize when you judge and be willing to practice a non-judgmental way of being and living. How will you shift yourself to walk your walk as an *open to all* kind of person, and spread that abundantly?

Open - Where it all starts!

 ay 26

BEING flexible means that you are open in your whole being; in your physical body with letting in health, in your mind with practicing positive and happy thoughts, in your soul by aligning with who you really are, and in consciousness through being one with all. How can you be more flexible—BE and live as an open energy?

Open - Where it all starts!

 Day 27

WHEN YOU ARE relaxed you are wide open—nothing is closed or blocked in you, for you, or as you. Breathe into this fact! Can you feel the absence of resistance or pressure in this allowing state? How will you consciously relax and make that open-ness your natural state?

Open - Where it all starts!

 ay 28

ENJOYING a happy life shows that you are open to experiencing bliss—otherwise, you would not have such fun. Sounds simple, yet sometimes it is challenging because we glue our happiness to the circumstances instead of the willing-ness to just be happy no matter what. How open are you to just being happy? How will you overcome your closed-ness to feel good? Now can you make yourself even wider to allow double the joy to carry you through your days?

Open - Where it all starts!

Day 29

It takes courage to trust in life and leave it the way it is. It also takes your open-ness to give your courage and trust the power they deserve. How will you give up the fight and, instead, let your boldness and knowing rule your world?

Open - Where it all starts!

 ay 30

ARE you looking for more adventures—small or big? How can you be more open to adventurous experiences in your life? What steps could you take to fly freely, openly, and be more excited about you being alive?

_____
_____
_____
_____
_____
_____
_____
_____
_____
_____
_____
_____
_____
_____
_____
_____
_____

Open - Where it all starts!

* * *

Ready to continue on your self-growth path? Get the next journal in this series: ***To BE and Live - The reason you are here!***

BONUS

Because hey, nobody ever wants the goodness to end.

Keep on opening!

Day 31

ALL YOUR SYMPTOMS - PHYSICAL, emotional, and energetic - are profound growing opportunities for you. The growth sits right in the middle of embracing and feeling them. Are you open to allowing yourself to fall in love with your symptoms, and also following their guidance?

Open - Where it all starts!

 ay 32

WHAT DO you want right now and how will you open up to receiving it? Make your *I-want-list* here!

___

Open - Where it all starts!

 ay 33

Being and living high-for-life is a state of open-ness—one that represents what you said you would do when you decided to come into your physicality. The ups and downs, and lefts and rights, are also part of that state—however, you promised yourself to BE and live in the open-ness of love while handling them. How will you claim your full open-ness, even in hard times, and fulfill your promise to yourself?

_____
_____
_____
_____
_____
_____
_____
_____
_____
_____
_____
_____
_____
_____
_____
_____
_____
_____
_____

Open - Where it all starts!

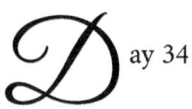 ay 34

NAY-SAYERS, negative-ers, and down-ers are closed to the full magic of being alive. So why would you even entangle yourself with them—closing yourself too? How will you stay in your magic, no matter if others have closed themselves and are walking closed through their lives?

_____
_____
_____
_____
_____
_____
_____
_____
_____
_____
_____
_____
_____
_____
_____
_____
_____
_____
_____
_____

Open - Where it all starts!

 ay 35

WHAT OPEN-NESS WOULD you act on if nobody would be watching? Might be a silly - or even dangerous - question, but I had to ask, and since this is your journal you can get really really truthful here. Go for it!

Open - Where it all starts!

AND NOW IT'S YOUR TURN!

The following are your magical pages to turn your own personal closed-ness into being open.

I'm counting on you to go wide here!

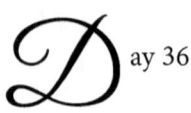 ay 36

OPEN-NESS IS...

___

Open - Where it all starts!

Day 37

OPEN-NESS IS...

Open - Where it all starts!

 Day 38

OPEN-NESS IS...

Open - Where it all starts!

Day 39

OPEN-NESS IS...

Open - Where it all starts!

 ay 40

Open-ness is...

Open - Where it all starts!

ALSO BY JACQUELINE PIRTLE

365 Days of Happiness

Because happiness is a piece of cake!

This passage book invites you to create a daily habit to live your every day joy, and is the parent companion to *365 Days of Happiness*, the journal workbook.

✳ ✳ ✳

365 Days of Happiness - **Special Edition**

Because happiness is a piece of cake

This beautiful Special Edition of the bestseller ***365 Days of Happiness: Because happiness is a piece of cake*** has room for your notes after every daily passage.

✳ ✳ ✳

365 Days of Happiness - **Journal Workbook**

This enlightening journal workbook is your daily tool to create a habit of living your every day bliss, and is the companion to ***365 Days of Happiness: Because happiness is a piece of cake.***

✳ ✳ ✳

Life IS Beautiful - Here's to New Beginnings

If you like digging deeper into the meaning of life and are inspired by spirituality, then you'll love Jacqueline's effective teachings.

✳ ✳ ✳

Parenting Through the Eyes of Lollipops

A Guide to Conscious Parenting

If you like harmony at home and laughter in the house, then you'll love Jacqueline's inspirational methods.

* * *

What it Means to BE a Woman

And Yes! Women do Poop!

If you like to live free, empowered, and want to decide for yourself, then you'll love Jacqueline's liberating ways.

* * *

What. If. - A 30 Day Journal

Turning your what IFs into it IS!

If you like to be in charge of your own life, turn your dreams into reality, enjoy journaling, and want to squeeze the most out of your time, then you'll love Jacqueline uplifting teachings.

* * *

What. If. - A 90 Day Journal - The Extended Edition

Turning your what IFs into it IS!

If you like to be in charge of your own life, turn your dreams into reality, enjoy journaling, and want to squeeze the most out of your time, then you'll love Jacqueline uplifting teachings.

ABOUT THE AUTHOR

Bestselling author, podcaster, and holistic practitioner, Jacqueline Pirtle, has twenty-four years of experience helping thousands of clients discover their own happiness. Jacqueline is the owner of *FreakyHealer* and has shared her solid teachings through her podcast *The Daily Freak*, sessions, workshops, presentations, and books with clients all over the world. She holds international degrees in holistic health and natural living. Her effective healing work has been featured in print and online magazines, podcasts, radio shows, on TV, and in the documentary *The Overly Emotional Child by Learning Success*, available on Amazon Prime.

For any questions you might have, to sign up for Jacqueline's newsletter, and for more information on whatever else she is up to, visit www.freakyhealer.com and her social media accounts @freakyhealer.

www.ingramcontent.com/pod-product-compliance
Lightning Source LLC
Chambersburg PA
CBHW071423070526
44578CB00003B/673